REMEMBERING THE FALLEN

OF THE

FIRST WORLD WAR

Sarah Ridley

FRANKLIN WATTS
LONDON•SYDNEY

Franklin Watts

First published in Great Britain in 2015 by The Watts Publishing Group

Editor: John C. Miles
Cover Designer: Peter Scoulding
Designer: Jason Billin

Picture credits: Second Lieutenant Thomas Keith Aitkin/IWM: 8, 13. By Kind Permission of the descendants of Harry Ayres/Bloxham Village Museum: 37. By Kind Permission of the descendants of Lionel Baker: 7b. By Kind Permission of the descendants of Maurice Baker: 44l. Ivan L Bawtree/ IWM: 16, 19. BJM/Alamy: 36t. John Bradley/Wikimedia Commons: 39. Lieutenant John Warwick Brooke/IWM: front cover main, 6b. Lieutenant Ernest Brooks/IWM: 5t, 12. By Kind Permission of Campbell College Belfast: 40t. Central Press/Getty Images: 28t. Paul Daniels/Shutterstock: back cover. Pavel Dudek/Shutterstock: 24b. By Kind Permission of the descendants of Charles Gasper: 33b. By Kind Permission of Suzanne Greenway: 4. By Kind Permission of Martin Haddrill/Pilton Church: 35tr. Brian Harris: 14c, 15 © 2008, 17t © 2006, 17b © 2014, 18, 20, 21, 23t © 2006, 23b, 25 © 2014, 41 © 2005. Angelo Hornak/Alamy: 31. Hulton Archive/Getty Images: 7t, 30b. ILN/Mary Evans PL: 32b. Imaake/Shutterstock: front cover b/g. Imperial War Museum, London: 6t, 10b, 11, 24t, 26t, 26b, 32t, 34, 42. IWM/Getty Images: 28b. By Kind Permission of Lavenham Church: 29, 36b. George P Lewis/IWM: 27. By Kind Permission of John C. Miles: 35bl, 38b, 40b. Jeff Morgan 01/Alamy: 33t. National Army Museum, London: 9. Peace Pledge Union: 43t. Sasha/Getty Images: 10t. By Kind Permission of the descendants of William and Robert Semple: 5b, 44r. Bob Speel: 38t. Topfoto: 22t. Topical Press/Getty Images: 30t. Vlas 2000/Shutterstock: 14b. Tony Watson/Alamy: 43b. Wikimedia Commons: 22b.

Dewey number: 940.3

HB ISBN 978 1 4451 4250 0

Library ebook ISBN 978 1 4451 4251 7

Printed in China

Franklin Watts
An imprint of
Hachette Children's Group
Part of The Watts Publishing Group
Carmelite House
50 Victoria Embankment
London EC4Y 0DZ

An Hachette UK Company
www.hachette.co.uk
www.franklinwatts.co.uk

Note to parents and teachers

Every effort has been made by the Publishers to ensure that the web sites in this book are suitable for children, that they are of the highest educational value, and that they contain no inappropriate or offensive material. However, because of the nature of the Internet, it is impossible to guarantee that the contents of these sites will not be altered. We strongly advise that Internet access is supervised by a responsible adult.

CONTENTS

FOR THE FALLEN

In the early months of the First World War, thousands died on both sides. Newspapers printed reports of the battles fought at Mons, Le Cateau and the River Marne. While on holiday in Cornwall, museum curator and poet, Laurence Binyon, had just been reading about the acts of heroism as well as the high loss of life in some of these early battles when he sat down to write his famous poem 'For the Fallen'. Its theme of remembrance resonated with people at the time and since, especially the fourth verse, which is intoned all across the world during remembrance services:

Laurence Binyon probably wrote his poem, 'For the Fallen', as he looked out at this view from Pentire Point, near Polzeath in Cornwall. The poem was printed in The Times *on 21 September 1914.*

They shall grow not old, as we that are left grow old:
Age shall not weary them, nor the years condemn.
At the going down of the sun and in the morning
We will remember them.

World war

Since the 28 June 1914 when Archduke Franz Ferdinand, heir to the Austro-Hungarian throne, was assassinated, country after country had declared war on each other. By the 4 August, Germany was already at war with Serbia, Russia and France – and now it found itself at war with Britain after the German army marched into Belgium in order to reach France. Over the next four years, battles took place across Europe, in areas of the Middle East and Africa, and out at sea, killing people at a previously unimaginable rate.

Like so many families, the Semples were in mourning when the war came to an end. Their eldest son, Second Lieutenant William Semple (bottom), died in June 1916 and their younger son, Captain Robert Semple (top), died on 5 November 1918.

This horse and wagon team carried supplies to the front line during the Battle of the Somme (July–November 1916). By this time, the landscape was scarred by individual burials and temporary cemeteries.

A huge cost

Over four years later, on 11 November 1918, the war came to an end. Britain and her allies were the victors and the ceasefire was a time for celebration across the British Empire, in France, Belgium and the USA, but it was also a difficult time. The war had been won at great cost in human lives. In all, around 16 million people had died worldwide of which almost 10 million were in the armed forces and over 6 million were civilians.

Grief and remembrance

A huge task lay ahead for the governments involved to clear the battlefields and establish cemeteries and memorials to the dead. For those who had lost loved ones, their attention turned to how to come to terms with their grief. The need to commemorate the dead led to memorials, monuments and acts of remembrance. This book will mainly focus on the ways that the British government and the British people set about honouring those who had fought and died during the war.

RECEIVING BAD NEWS

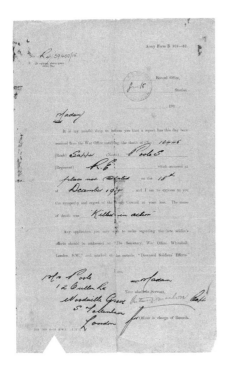

'It is my painful duty to inform you that a report has this day been received from the War Office notifying the death of No 10445 Sapper Poole S of the Royal Engineers...'

Army Form B104-82

Each individual death during the war represented a tragedy for the family waiting for news back at home. More than one million servicemen and women from the British Empire died, of which the majority were soldiers in the British army.

Back in Britain, Post Office messenger boys delivered telegrams announcing the death of an army officer while the families of men or women below the rank of officer received a formal letter – Army Form B104-82. Sometimes relatives heard the news first from letters written by friends serving alongside the deceased.

Many soldiers wrote final letters, addressed to their wife, girlfriend or mother. These letters were tucked into their pocket book with their will, or were left with someone who was not involved in the attack whose duty it became to post the letters if the soldiers were killed. Whether someone died of illness, during an attack or was picked off by a lone sniper, those serving alongside tried their best to ensure that the personal possessions of the dead person were sent back to their families.

Men of the Royal Army Medical Corps search the backpacks of dead soldiers for letters or other personal effects to return to their families after the Battle of Guillemont, 1916.

Vera Brittain

In her famous memoir, *Testament of Youth*, Vera Brittain recalled the horror of the moment when her dead fiancé's family unwrapped a parcel containing his muddy and blood-stained uniform and other personal possessions. Her fiancé, Roland Leighton, had been fatally wounded in December 1915, just hours before he was due to come home on leave. Vera searched the uniform for any last messages but only found some poems. The family buried the uniform in the garden.

A long wait

For some families, it was a long wait. They received an official letter informing them that their soldier was missing, giving the date when their relative was last seen alive. This might mean that he was a prisoner of war or had become separated from his regiment – or he might be lying injured in a hospital. People wrote letters to the commanding officer, to field hospitals, to the Red Cross and anyone who had known their relative, asking for any more information. Some families placed adverts in newspapers appealing for information relating to their missing person. After six months, if there was no further news, the army officially registered them as missing, presumed dead. The families of dead airmen and sailors heard the news in similar ways.

Vera Brittain, who volunteered to become a Red Cross VAD nurse during the war, suffered the tragedy of losing her fiancé, two close friends and her brother – all soldiers killed during the war.

This telegram from the War Office dated 8 April 1918 must have caused terrible anxiety for the Baker family with its message: 'Regret Capt L J Baker Suffolk Regt att (attached) Second Batt (Battalion) missing March twenty eight. No details known.'

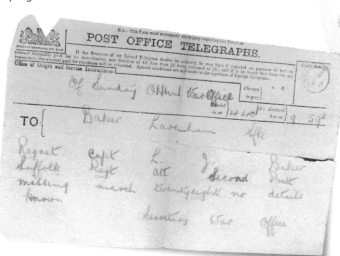

Fortunately, the Red Cross sent a telegram on 18 April 1918 relaying this news: 'Happy to inform you your son reported prisoner. Writing.' Captain L J Baker was a prisoner of war in Germany. He spent the rest of the war as a prisoner and returned home safely.

BURYING A COMRADE

When a soldier, sailor or airman died during the First World War, they were buried close to where they had died. Unlike today, there was no tradition of bringing the bodies back for burial at home.

The funeral of German pilot, Manfred von Richthofen. Known as the Red Baron, he was buried with full military honours by the Australian army in April 1918.

Soldiers who died in the trenches or on the battlefield were buried by their comrades in hastily dug graves or in cemeteries further back from the front line. Some were buried in mass graves, created by digging a long trench in the earth. If the padre (army chaplain) was available, he conducted a short burial service. Sometimes, an officer simply said a few prayers over the body before covering it over with earth.

Thousands of graves were created in the first months of the war. When they could, soldiers put up a wooden cross carrying the name of the dead soldier, or marked the spot, hoping to return with a cross at a later time. Cemeteries sprang up behind the front line and close to hospitals to bury those who had died from wounds or illness.

Burying the enemy

Soldiers on both sides buried the bodies of their enemies too. If they could identify them, they wrote their names on a grave marker; if not, they might just write 'French soldier' or 'German soldier'. When the Red Baron, the ace German fighter pilot, was killed in action on 21 April 1918, he was buried with full military honours (see photo). Members of the Australian Flying Corps fired a gun salute over his grave during the funeral.

A growing problem

In the early months of the war, no one was keeping a record of the everyday burials, which were at risk of being lost as a result of further fighting in the area. Men working for a Red Cross ambulance unit had already taken on the task of helping families find information about soldiers listed as 'missing' and now they began to note down where men were buried as well, and even started to care for their graves.

Meanwhile, back at home, there was growing pressure that officials should do something about the graves of the thousands of men who were dying in the armed services. Some people called for the repatriation of the bodies; they wanted to bring their loved ones back home, for proper funerals and burial in cemeteries and churchyards close to members of the family.

After a battle, battlefield cemeteries were created for the dead. Here a soldier tends the grave of one of the almost 4,000 men of the 38th Welsh Division who were killed in July 1916 during five days of fighting close to the River Somme.

FABIAN WARE AND THE GRAVES REGISTRATION COMMISSION

Fabian Ware was 45 when war broke out. He had been a journalist and a teacher but now he volunteered to take charge of a Red Cross ambulance unit that was searching French villages for missing soldiers in the early months of the war.

Ware was horrified to see that there was no official system for registering the death and burial of soldiers on the Western Front. He could see that the lack of an official system would make it extremely difficult for families to locate and visit the graves of their loved ones when the war was over.

The Graves Registration Commission

In March 1915, in recognition of the informal burial registration that his volunteers were already carrying out, the British army put Ware in charge of a small team of nine men to work under the title of the Graves Registration Commission (GRC). Their work had two main aims: to establish a register of the graves of officers and men, noting down which had crosses or inscriptions, and create a second register giving the geographical location of each grave. The French government also established an organisation to register burials in 1915.

A portrait of Fabian Ware, taken in 1920.

Between May and October 1915, a growing number of men working for Graves Registration Units registered over 31,000 graves. The men interviewed chaplains and checked hospital records to help identify each dead soldier. If none existed, wooden crosses were erected recording the name and army number of the dead man.

The wooden cross marking the grave of Lance Corporal A G Baker was photographed and sent to his family by the GRC. The photo card included useful information about the location of the grave, should the family want to visit at a future date.

Before long, grieving relatives started to write letters to the GRC, often requesting a photograph of the grave. It was extremely difficult for bereaved families as, without a body, they could not hold a funeral service and follow the usual rituals of mourning. Ware decided to respond to these family requests for photographs of the graves and the Red Cross paid for the cost of photographers, prints and cards (see example bottom of page 10).

Alongside the grave registration work, Fabian Ware started talks with the French government to acquire land for British military cemeteries. The French government offered land as well as care of the graves. The British government gratefully accepted the gift of the land but decided to care for the graves themselves.

The issue of repatriation

During the early months of the war, a few families paid for the bodies of their sons or husbands to be brought back from France. Ware was against this as he recognised that only the wealthy could afford to do so. In addition he listened to the views of many officers in the army, many of whom said they would want to be buried with their men. In March 1915 the British army decreed that all soldiers who died in a war zone had to be buried with their comrades, close to where they had died.

Names were recorded on wooden crosses in pencil or paint. Later on, a machine was used to punch out the name of the dead man and his army service number on an aluminium strip, which was nailed to the cross.

THE IMPERIAL WAR GRAVES COMMISSION, 1917

Britain's declaration of war against Germany in 1914 had brought thousands of troops from across the British Empire to fight in war zones in Europe and elsewhere. At the Imperial Conference held in March 1917, it was agreed that the Imperial War Graves Commission (IWGC) should be established to care for their graves.

Established by Royal Charter on 21 May 1917, the first meeting of the Imperial War Graves Commission (which changed its name to the Commonwealth War Graves Commission in 1960) took place in November of that year. Its role was to care for all members of the armed forces of the British Empire who 'died from wounds inflicted, accident occurring or disease contracted, while on active service whether on sea or land'. The Commission was to obtain land for cemeteries and memorials, erect and maintain headstones and memorials, keep records and look after individual graves that were not inside cemeteries.

The 20th Deccan Horse of the Indian army, prior to an unsuccessful attack on High Wood on 14 July 1916, during the Battle of the Somme. Over one million Indians served in the First World War.

Equal treatment in death

At the first meeting, General Macready of the British army expressed his desire that 'in the erection of memorials on the graves there should be no distinction between officers and men'. There would be no mass graves for ordinary soldiers and memorials for officers, as was usual in the past, but equal treatment for all.

Cemetery design

Discussions began about how the cemeteries should be laid out. Fabian Ware, as vice chairman of the IWGC, asked leading architects Edwin Lutyens and Herbert Baker for their recommendations but they had very different visions. Eventually Sir Frederic Kenyon, director of the British Museum, was asked to act as the overall advisor to the Commission on the design of the cemeteries.

Nurses, members of the Women's Army Auxiliary Corps (WAACs) and other female volunteers who died abroad were buried with the same reverence as servicemen. This photo shows the funeral of a nurse killed during an air raid on a hospital in Étaples, France in 1918.

Kenyon's recommendations became the blueprint for the cemeteries. His vision was that 'the general appearance of a British cemetery will be that of an enclosure with plots of grass or flowers (or both) separated by paths of varying size, and set with orderly rows of headstones, uniform in height and width.' Graves should face east and cemeteries should include a large 'altar' stone, a stone cross and a building where the register of graves could be kept safe. He recommended that Herbert Baker, Edwin Lutyens and Reginald Blomfield should be the senior architects.

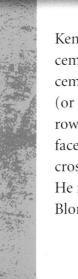

CEMETERY DESIGN
AND FEATURES

Architects and garden designers began work immediately, designing memorials and advising on which plants to use.

In 1917, Reginald Blomfield designed the Cross of Sacrifice to represent the Christian faith of the majority of the men, and of their families. It is a simple stone cross with a bronze sword running down its shaft, set on an octagonal base. The cross represents the sacrifice that the men had made for God and for everyone, and the sword represents war.

Reginald Blomfield's Cross of Sacrifice stands in all CWGC cemeteries with 40 graves or more, unless the majority of the men buried there followed a faith other than Christianity. The stone cross was built to different dimensions, depending on the size of the cemetery.

By contrast, Edwin Lutyens' 'great stone' as he called it, aimed to represent people of all faiths. His idea became the Stone of Remembrance, a large rectangular block of white Portland stone with three steps leading up to it that can be found in the larger cemeteries. Some people see it as a memorial stone, others as an altar. Carved in large letters on both sides of the monument are the words: THEIR NAME LIVETH FOR EVERMORE, words chosen by Rudyard Kipling (see page 16) from the Bible.

A Stone of Remembrance.

Cemetery register and gardens

So that visitors could read the names of the men or women buried in the cemetery or remembered on the memorials to the missing, a cemetery register was to be created for each cemetery. In larger cemeteries, architects designed a shelter building for the register, where people would be able to rest out of the weather, and in smaller ones the register was to be kept in a brass register box. There would also be a map of the burial plots, to aid identification.

From the beginning, the IWGC wanted to make the cemeteries places of beauty and peace and so garden design was at the centre of their plans. Gertrude Jekyll, a friend of Lutyens and a respected garden designer, was one of the experts called on to advise on design and planting. Following her advice, IWGC gardeners planted roses and low-growing plants to create the feeling of a cottage garden or country churchyard.

The CWGC employs 900 gardeners worldwide to maintain and care for the grass, trees and plants in the cemeteries.

THE HEADSTONES

At the very first meeting of the Imperial War Graves Commission in 1917 it was decided that the headstones should be the same, regardless of rank or religion.

Equality in death was the guiding principle that ran through all the work of the Imperial War Graves Commission. Each headstone would be engraved with the name, rank and regiment of the deceased, as well as the date of death. Relatives would be allowed to add a short inscription or prayer, so long as it had the approval of the Commission and was no longer than four lines long.

Experts were consulted on every detail of the headstones. The Royal Geological Society recommended the use of Portland stone or Hopton Wood limestone for the cemeteries in France and Belgium as these stones were good quality, long-lasting and affordable. In Italy the headstones are made of a local stone and in Turkey the headstones have a low shape to withstand earthquakes and the harsh climate.

Inscriptions

Rudyard Kipling, the literary advisor to the Commission, used his writing skills to come up with this simple but poignant inscription for the headstones of unidentified men:

A SOLDIER OF THE GREAT WAR KNOWN UNTO GOD.

Kipling knew how important it was to families of the bereaved that unidentified soldiers should have a headstone since his only son, John, was wounded and listed as 'missing' at the Battle of Loos in 1915. Kipling spent several years searching for his son's corpse without success. In 1992, the CWGC were finally able to name a previously unidentified soldier as John Kipling, and changed the headstone accordingly.

Each headstone included the badge of the dead man's unit, for instance a maple leaf for Canadians, as here, or a kowhai frond for New Zealanders. At first skilled craftsmen carved each headstone by hand. Later, machines were used to speed up the process of inscribing the regimental badges.

Headstone shape

After some debate, the Commission decided on a rounded headstone rather than a cross for two main reasons. The shape allowed more words within the space and it was suitable for the dead of all religions, rather than just Christians, in recognition of the fact that the cemeteries would hold people of all faiths including Muslims, Jews and Hindus.

The Commission was dedicated to the idea of naming each identified soldier and raising a headstone, as well as raising a headstone for each unidentified body. Other countries were taking different decisions, including the French who eventually decided to place the bones of unidentified soldiers in huge sculptural ossuaries.

A few headstones represent more than one soldier, usually because their corpses were so close together that it was difficult to separate them.

The Battle of Verdun lasted for most of 1916 and claimed thousands of French and German lives. The bodies of identified soldiers were buried with stone cross markers in the French National Cemetery at Douaument. The bones of unidentified soldiers lie inside the vast ossuary with its stone tower, seen in the distance.

WAR OVER, WORK AHEAD

When the guns fell silent, the work of the Commission could begin in earnest.

Since 1915, when the French government had agreed to donate land to the British for the burial of their soldiers, thousands of servicemen and a few women had been buried in military cemeteries laid out according to French rules: graves were to be placed 23–30 cm apart and a path not wider than 90 cm wide was to be laid between the rows of graves. Now these cemeteries needed to be turned into the final resting places of the dead, with memorials, gardens and stone headstones to replace the wooden grave markers.

In front of the Cross of Sacrifice at Tyne Cot Military Cemetery, Belgium, you can see the original burials and behind the cross you can see rows of later burials. Almost 12,000 graves were eventually laid out in this, the biggest CWGC cemetery.

Graves Concentration Units

There were also numerous isolated graves as well as clusters of graves representing the army policy of burying men close to where they had died. The Commission decided that, where possible, if a battlefield cemetery contained ten graves or more, it would become the focus for a new cemetery and other isolated burials would be exhumed and moved to the new cemetery. This work was to be carried out under the control of Graves Concentration Units.

Clearing the battlefields

But first workers needed to clear the battlefields of military equipment and bodies, a grim task carried out by the army using soldiers and men in the Army Labour Corps, working with the Graves Registration Units and Graves Concentration Units. They always tried to identify the dead, searching for identification discs or tags, scraps of uniform, personal items or even distinguishing features. The body remains were then carried to the designated cemetery and buried in marked graves or unmarked graves.

Soldiers working for the Commission created Body Density Maps that recorded cemeteries and the location of the dead. The maps were used to help find and, where necessary, move and rebury soldiers' bodies. Over 200,000 bodies were moved from battlefields to cemeteries between the end of the war and September 1921.

First cemeteries completed

The Commission completed three cemeteries in 1920 to try out all the decisions that had been made so far about the design and layout of the cemeteries. Blomfield's design for the Forceville Cemetery Extension in France was seen to address the Commission's ideas (see page 13) the most successfully. Only one year later in the spring of 1921, 1,000 cemeteries were ready to receive visitors although most of them did not have stone headstones for several more years.

Battlefields were systematically searched several times by groups of men. It was distressing work, gathering bodies and body parts for removal to the designated cemetery.

The rights of the relatives

Meanwhile, the Commission's vision for the dead of the war was challenged by relatives of the dead, some of whom continued to fight for the right to bring back the bodies of their loved ones. Others wanted the right to erect headstones of their own choice and design. In 1920, a petition of more than 8,000 signatures was presented to Edward, the Prince of Wales, patron of the IWGC, asking for the right to erect a Christian cross. These issues were debated in Parliament in May 1920 where the Commission's plans for uniformity of headstones and non-repatriation of the dead were finally accepted.

The uniformity of the headstones was a crucial part of the Commission's vision for the cemeteries (see page 13). In fact many families chose to have a Christian cross engraved on the headstone but it was not compulsory.

Across in France, similar discussions about repatriation had been going on during the war and since it ended. In 1920, the government eventually gave in to pressure from families and allowed them to bring bodies back 'home'. Out of about 700,000 identified bodies, 300,000 were transported back to their family homes for re-burial.

Uniform, but not identical

Back in England, although the Commission wanted the military cemeteries to look very similar, the architect of each cemetery was free to design the cemetery to fit in with existing landscape features and to reflect the nationality of the majority of the people buried there. For instance, at Noyelles-sur-Mer Cemetery in France, 841 men of the Chinese Labour Corps are buried. These men had helped to dig trenches and move supplies, and also helped clear the battlefields after the war. To respect their culture, a pine tree was planted in place of a Cross of Sacrifice and the entrance arch reflects Chinese architecture. The headstones are inscribed with the name of each worker in Chinese characters, with an English translation underneath.

Early on in the process, the Commission realised it had set itself an enormous task. Over 1,000 gardeners were at work in France in 1921, sowing grass, laying paths, and planting trees and shrubs. In 1923 alone, 4,000 headstones a week were being sent to France. It took until 1938 to replace all the wooden crosses with headstones and erect all the memorials. A year later, another world war began.

At Noyelles-sur-Mer Chinese Cemetery in France the Commission's gardeners planted Lebanese cedars, pine trees and chrysanthemums, which are all native to China.

THE MISSING

After the war, there were hundreds of thousands of servicemen with no known grave. Their loved ones found this situation extremely distressing. Some even suggested that a headstone bearing their son's name could be set up over an empty grave.

The Commission wanted to give these men the same respect as those with a grave and a headstone and, to this end, they commissioned a number of memorials to the missing to be erected in significant locations relating to campaigns during the war.

The Menin Gate

The first to be commissioned was the Menin Gate Memorial in Ypres, Belgium, designed by Reginald Blomfield. The site was chosen because so many men had marched through the original Menin Gate on their way to and from the battlefields. The names of more than 54,000 men are engraved on the memorial, men who lost their lives in the area up until 16 August 1917 but have no known grave. When Field Marshal Lord Plumer unveiled the memorial in 1927 he spoke these words of consolation to the crowd: 'He is not missing. He is here.'

A crowd gathered to witness the unveiling of the Menin Gate Memorial on 24 July 1927, while people at home in Britain listened to the BBC radio broadcast of the event.

Sir Edwin Lutyens.

Thiepval Memorial

Meanwhile, Sir Edward Lutyens was working on another memorial to the missing – the Thiepval Memorial to the Missing of the Somme. This huge abstract monument sits on a ridge of land that was fought over during the battle and commemorates more than 72,000 men with no known grave who died in the Somme area between July 1916 and March 1918. More than 90 per cent of the men commemorated on this memorial died during the Battle of the Somme (July–November 1916).

National memorials

Some of the memorials were incorporated into the design of an IWGC cemetery. At Lone Pine Cemetery in Turkey, the Australian government decided to build a memorial on the site of some of the fiercest fighting in 1915 where thousands of lives were lost on both sides. The memorial commemorates more than 4,900 Australian and New Zealand servicemen who died trying to capture the Gallipoli Peninsula and who have no known grave.

Many of the countries in the British Empire built national memorials to the dead during the 1920s and 1930s. Out of the 625,000 Canadians who went to war, 60,000 died. The Canadian Battlefields Memorial Commission decided to raise a monument to all the Canadians who fought in the war as well as to the 11,000 Canadians with no known grave.

The Lone Pine Memorial to the Missing stands at one end of Lone Pine Cemetery in Turkey. It gets its name from a single pine tree that was still standing at the beginning of the fighting in mid-1915, but was soon obliterated.

The Canadian National Vimy Memorial was unveiled by King Edward VIII in 1936 and stands on Vimy Ridge in France, which four divisions of the Canadian Corps captured on 9 April 1917 during the Battle of Arras.

PILGRIMAGES
AND BATTLEFIELD TOURS

Pilgrims who were taking part in the British Legion Pilgrimage in 1928 were photographed eating lunch in a shell hole at Vimy Ridge, France. Several of them are wearing medals.

Thousands of families and ex-servicemen made pilgrimages to the former war zones in the years after the war had ended.

Even while the war was still raging, some French and British people managed to obtain a special pass from military authorities in order to travel to France or Belgium and visit the graves of their relatives. This was only possible if the grave was sufficiently behind the front line.

Pilgrimages

Visiting the grave of a loved one helped people come to terms with their loss. If they could afford it, people travelled from as far away as Canada or Australia to visit the grave or memorial engraved with their relative's name. In Britain, the Saint Barnabas Society was founded in 1919 to enable less wealthy people to make pilgrimages, offering group tours at a fraction of the price of more commercial trips. Ten years after the war had ended, 11,000 ex-servicemen and women and other relatives took part in a huge British Legion Battlefield Pilgrimage which included a service at Menin Gate.

Since 11 November 1929, members of Ypres' fire brigade have played the Last Post at the entrance to the Menin Gate Memorial at 8pm every evening – apart from during the Second World War (1939–45). Watching the ceremony has become part of many people's battlefield tour (see right).

Battlefield tourism

Alongside the pilgrimages, battlefield tourism developed – aided by guidebooks produced by Michelin. Now known as remembrance or battlefield tourism, people continue to visit cemeteries, memorials and museums but the battlefields have long since been returned to farming or other uses.

Visitors to the cemeteries of the Western Front today will usually visit British cemeteries as well as German and French ones. People are encouraged to note the differences between the cemeteries built by the French, the British and the Germans. As the defeated nation, the Germans had fewer choices and were given considerably less space for their cemeteries in France and Belgium. In the mid 1920s work began on German military cemeteries, moving burials from other sites into a small number of cemeteries. As a result of the space issue, many Germans lie buried in mass graves in cemeteries designed to fit in with the local landscape.

Langemark German Military Cemetery was established during the war but was massively expanded during the 1930s, when about 10,000 men were reburied here. The statue of the four mourning soldiers, seen here in the distance, was erected after the Second World War.

Peace Day and
The Cenotaph

The fighting came to an end with a ceasefire at 11 o'clock on 11 November 1918 but it took until 28 June 1919 for the war to officially end when the peace treaty was signed at Versailles, France.

At the Paris Peace Conference in early 1919, 32 countries gathered to work out the terms of the peace treaty. The negotiations were difficult and went on for months. The terms of the Versailles Treaty were harsh and caused German officials to protest that they were unfair. Ultimately, however, Germany had little choice but to sign. Meanwhile the British government started to plan a public celebration of the official end to the war – a Peace Day on 19 July 1919.

Peace Day preparations

London was to be the focus for the celebrations. Some in government felt that it would be better to spend the money supporting ex-servicemen, some of whom had fallen on hard times or were disabled by war wounds, but plans went ahead for a huge military parade through the capital. Prime Minister David Lloyd George wanted the people involved in the Victory Parade to pause and pay homage to the war dead so he asked Sir Edwin Lutyens to design a temporary monument to the dead. The memorial needed to be ready in just two weeks, which might have been impossible if Lutyens hadn't already been sketching out designs for memorials to the dead. His idea for a cenotaph, which means 'empty tomb' in Greek, was accepted and built in wood and plaster on Whitehall, central London, ready for the Victory Parade.

Lutyens' original sketches for the Cenotaph.

Peace Day Parade

Thousands of people flocked to London to line the streets of the parade route on 19 July and rejoice that the war was officially over. Almost 15,000 servicemen took part in the parade and saluted the Cenotaph, dedicated to 'The Glorious Dead', as they passed. What happened next surprised the government. The Cenotaph became a place of pilgrimage for the bereaved, who laid wreaths and bunches of flowers in memory of those who had died during the war. The government was forced to leave it standing and to replace it with a permanent stone memorial, unveiled on Armistice Day 1920 (see page 28).

Members of the public crowded around the Cenotaph after the military Victory Parade had passed on Peace Day, 19 July 1919. Almost immediately members of the public started to leave flowers around the base of the monument.

ARMISTICE DAY AND REMEMBRANCE SUNDAY

A year after the war ended, the first commemoration of the end of the war established many of the traditions that continue today.

As the clock reached 11 o'clock on 11 November 1919, the whole of Britain came to a halt for two minutes of silence. This idea had been suggested by Edward Honey, an Australian journalist working in London, and was taken up by King George V who wrote: 'All locomotion should cease, so that, in perfect stillness, the thoughts of everyone may be concentrated on reverent remembrance of the glorious dead.'

At 11 o'clock on 11 November 1919, shoppers and workers on Oxford Street, London, were photographed marking the first two-minute silence.

A nation remembers

A service of remembrance was held at the Cenotaph. Crowds watched leading politicians and members of the armed forces lay wreaths and ex-servicemen paraded past, paying their respects to 'The Glorious Dead'. At the same time church services were held throughout the country as the nation stopped to mourn the dead of the war. The following year, 11 November 1920, King George V unveiled the permanent stone Cenotaph at a ceremony on his way to Westminster Abbey, where the unknown warrior was to be laid to rest (see pages 30–31). Crowds of onlookers watched the unveiling, many of them dressed in black.

The Cenotaph, originally made in plaster and wood, was remade in Portland stone and unveiled on 11 November 1920.

Armistice Balls

In the years immediately after the war, Armistice Day was also a time for veterans to celebrate their survival at parties or Armistice Balls held at the grandest London hotels. Elsewhere ex-servicemen were more likely to meet friends at the local branch of the British Legion or in a pub. By the mid 1920s, public opinion was turning to disapproval of these celebrations to mark the end of the war and gradually they died out.

Remembrance Sunday

During 1920 and 1921, thousands of war memorials were unveiled across the country. On 11 November, most of the local community attended services based around war memorials, as recalled by the vicar of Lavenham Church in Suffolk, writing in the 1920s: 'A United Service is held on each Armistice Day, and each year the church is crowded. The Last Post is sounded, and wreaths are brought up one by one and handed to the rector, who lays them on the War Memorial… It is hoped the Armistice Day will always be observed as a day of proud remembrance and of high resolve.' After the Second World War, the second Sunday in November, Remembrance Sunday, took over from 11 November as the national day of remembrance for the dead of both world wars and of subsequent conflicts. Today Armistice Day itself is also known as Remembrance Day or Poppy Day.

The names of the 76 men commemorated on the war memorial in Lavenham Church in Suffolk are still read out at remembrance services, as they have been since 1920, when the memorial was unveiled.

THE TOMB OF THE
UNKNOWN WARRIOR

The Tomb of the Unknown Warrior lies in Westminster Abbey, London. It is one of the most visited war graves in the world.

The idea for the tomb came from Reverend David Railton, an army chaplain who served in France. In 1916 he noticed a grave in the garden of the house where he was staying and on the wooden grave marker were the words 'An Unknown British Soldier'. The sight moved him and stayed in his memory, eventually developing into this idea: that the body of an unidentified soldier should be brought back to Britain and reburied to act as a memorial to all the dead of the British Empire with no known grave.

After the war ended, Reverend Railton tried to get people interested in his idea. When he wrote to the Dean of Westminster Abbey, Herbert Ryle, in August 1920, Ryle took up his idea. It was decided that the body of an unknown soldier would be reburied in the nave of Westminster Abbey during a special service to be held on 11 November 1920.

Much to organise

There was much to organise and only a few months to do it. It was important to all who were involved that any clues as to the identity of the corpse should remain a secret. So the bodies of four unidentified soldiers were dug up from the four main areas of combat on the Western Front. One was selected and placed in a coffin while the other three were reburied.

On the morning of 11 November, 1920, two years after the war had ended, the coffin was carried through the streets of London on a gun carriage. Crowds of people lined the route as the coffin travelled first to the Cenotaph (see page 31) on Whitehall, where the stone memorial was unveiled by King George V, and then on to Westminster Abbey.

With great respect, the coffin containing the unknown warrior, now resting inside another oak coffin made from a tree that had grown in the grounds of Hampton Court Palace, was carried from its resting place in France to travel by carriage, boat and train to London.

The service

At Westminster Abbey a burial service was held. The congregation included many widows and grieving mothers whose sons or husbands had died during the war. In the week following, about 1,250,000 people filed past the grave to pay their respects. For many there was just a chance that it was their son, brother or husband who lay inside. For others it served as a focus for their grief. A week later, the grave was filled in with soil from the battlefields of France.

Around the world

At the same time as the unknown warrior was being buried in London, an unknown soldier was buried under the Arc de Triomphe in Paris, France. In 1921 the governments of Belgium, Italy, Portugal and the USA organised their own ceremonies around the burial of an unknown soldier. Much more recently, in the 1990s and 2000s, the governments of Australia, Canada and New Zealand have buried their own unknown soldiers.

At the Cenotaph, King George V laid a wreath of roses and bay leaves on the coffin, with a handwritten card that read: 'In proud memory of those warriors who died unknown in the great war. Unknown, and yet well known; as dying, and behold they live.' George RI

Today you can visit the tomb and read the words of the Dean of Westminster, Herbert Ryle, inscribed on a slab of black Belgian marble that was placed there in 1921.

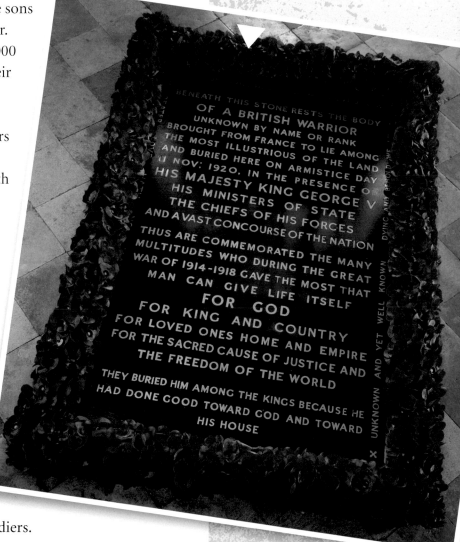

SHRINES AND ROLLS OF HONOUR

While the war was still going on, some communities created shrines and rolls of honour.

Servicemen and women were always in the thoughts of their families, friends and relatives. In the borough of Hackney in east London in 1916, the inhabitants of certain streets took this a step further and erected wooden street shrines. These held lists of the people in the street or streets who were serving in the armed forces and sometimes a separate list of those who had died. Street shrines became increasingly common across Britain.

The street shrine in Acton Lane, London, was on the outside wall of the local church. The photo shows a service that took place there in November 1916, perhaps to remember men who had died that year during the Battle of the Somme.

The shrines presented a problem for some members of the Church of England who saw them as places of superstition or even idolatry but the Bishop of Stepney thought they were a proper way for a community to recognise the efforts of men in the armed forces and also saw that they provided a focus for bereaved people. He conducted services of blessing at the shrines, which often drew together people of all faiths. After the war, some of the wooden shrines were incorporated into war memorials.

The Bishop of London created the largest shrine of them all in Hyde Park, London, which opened on 4 August 1918. The memorial was dedicated to all who were serving, had served or had been killed in the war.

Rolls of honour

Framed handwritten rolls of honour, listing all those from a local community who were serving in the armed forces, took pride of place in village halls, churches and chapels and again helped to keep those people in the minds and the prayers of the local community. The lists often needed to be updated as the war wore on. After the war, regiments, workplaces, schools and universities created permanent rolls of honour in the form of wooden boards or stone memorials. These listed all those from the school, workplace or regiment who had died on active service during the war. Some rolls of honour list all those who served and survived, as well as those that died.

Private shrines

On a domestic level, thousands of women created private shrines to sons, husbands or brothers who had died during the war or who were still fighting. Set on a mantelpiece or sideboard, this might include a framed photo of the loved one dressed in their uniform, a vase of fresh flowers and perhaps some personal possessions sent back from the war. After the war, families kept letters, medals and the memorial plaques with accompanying scroll and King's message sent to the next-of-kin of those who had died on active service. The idea behind the memorial plaques was to commemorate those that had died and acknowledge their sacrifice.

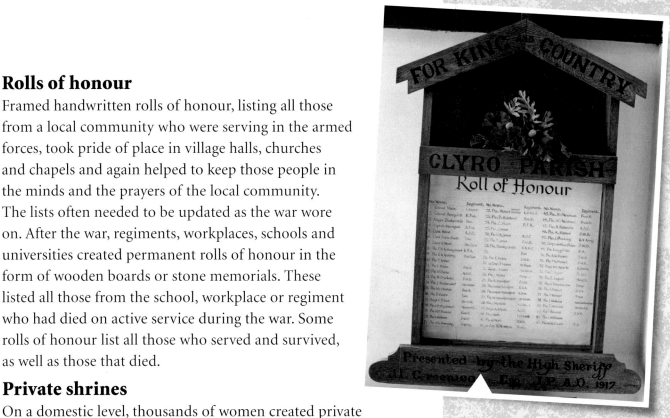

The Roll of Honour for the village of Clyro, Powys, Wales can still be seen in the porch of the village church.

Next-of-kin memorial plaques and scrolls were sent out to people across the British Empire who had lost servicemen or women during the war. This memorial plaque commemorates Private Charles Gasper of the Wiltshire Regiment who died in 1917 in Palestine, leaving a widow and a 15-month-old son whom he had never met.

RURAL
WAR MEMORIALS

In villages and rural communities across the country, relatives, friends and neighbours joined together to support each other when bereavement struck during the war years. After the war, people's thoughts turned to how to commemorate those that would never return.

Families had been unable to hold funerals due to the official policy of non-repatriation of bodies (see pages 11 and 20) so it is not that surprising that a popular movement to build war memorials sprang up in almost every village across the country. A war memorial created a place where people could grieve as a community, or alone. War memorial committees were established to discuss what form the memorial should take, who was to be commemorated, how to raise the money and who would deal with architects, stonemasons and builders.

The war memorial at Boughton Aluph, Kent, was unveiled in February 1921, as recorded here. Many war memorials were unveiled in the early 1920s and almost all were built using money raised by the local community.

IN
MEMORY OF
THE MEN
FROM THIS
PARISH
WHO DIED IN
THE SERVICE
OF THEIR
COUNTRY
DURING THE
GREAT WAR
1914—1918.

PERCY AMOS	EDWARD BRUNGA
CHARLES BROTHERWOOD	JAMES GREENSTREE
ERNEST BURCHETT	CHRISTOPHER HOOK
WILLIAM BAKER	ERNEST HUMPHBEY
HENRY BISHOPP	THOMAS HUCKSTEPP
FRANK HUCKSTEPP	CHARLES MERTON
FRANK LADD	WILLIAM NORRIS
RICHARD LADD	JOHN NEWPORT
CECIL MARTIN	FRANK POCKNELL
PERCY MERTON	ALFRED REYNOLDS
CHARLES STEBBINGS	GEORGE WILLIAMS
WILLIAM STRINGER	PERCY WILLIAMS
WILLIAM SINDEN	ERNEST WILSON
GEORGE VIDLER	HERBERT HODGE

"MAKE THEM TO BE NUMBERED WITH THY

War memorials of all types

Many war memorials are located in or close to parish churches or chapels. During the war, local clergymen visited bereaved families to offer their support and may have read out the names of the dead during Sunday services. Stone or brass plaques engraved with the names of the fallen were a popular choice for memorials inside churches and chapels although in some villages they spent the money on a memorial window (see right).

In other places, the villagers decided on a memorial in a public place, such as by the roadside or on the village green. Sculptors and stonemasons were commissioned to create stone crosses, obelisks or columns with the names of the dead engraved around the base. The unveiling ceremony often served as a form of funeral service for all those whose names were engraved on the memorial.

'This window is placed here to the Glory of God and in Memory of the men from this Parish (39 in all) who lost their lives in the Great War 1914–1918.' The war memorial window in Pilton Church in Devon features religious scenes as well as images of a sailor, a nurse, a member of the air force and a soldier.

The Celtic cross had become a popular choice for gravestones and memorials during the Victorian era. At West Firle in Sussex the war memorial to the ten men of Firle takes this form.

Less usual, but still quite widespread, are war memorials that served a practical purpose: a memorial hall (village hall), sports pavilion, remembrance garden, recreation ground, bus shelter, clock tower or schoolroom. These spaces were created for use by everyone and were built in memory of those that had died.

In the village of Lenham in Kent there was some debate about how to commemorate the 42 men of their village who were killed during the war. The local schoolteacher suggested that it should be a huge chalk cross, picked out on the hillside above the village. This idea was adopted and Mr C H Groom, the schoolteacher, designed a small garden of remembrance, a bench and a memorial stone engraved with the names of the dead as well.

Remembrance Sunday services were held out on the hillside at Lenham in Kent. In 1977, the memorial stone carved with the names of the dead was moved to the churchyard so that relatives who were getting too old to climb the hill could still visit it.

The Lavenham Book of Remembrance was produced by the vicar, Rev Lenox-Conyngham, and placed on a wooden memorial table beneath the war memorial (see page 29) in 1922.

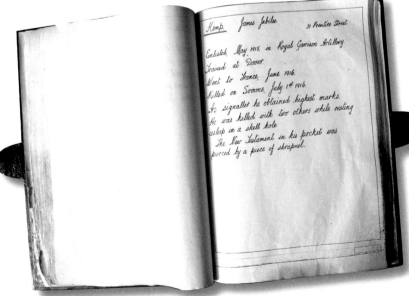

William Lever commissioned and paid for the memorial erected to the memory of over 500 men who worked for Lever brothers and who died during the war. It was built in Port Sunlight, the model village built by the Lever Brothers for employees of the Sunlight Soap Factory, and it includes unusual sculptures. There are images of women and children being defended by soldiers, as well as soldiers helping wounded or dying comrades.

Book of remembrance

Another form of war memorial is a book of remembrance. While many books contain handwritten lists of all who died from the local community, others contain more information. In 1922, the vicar of Lavenham collected biographical information about all the men listed on the war memorial, so that '… something, more than their mere names, may be known of the Lavenham men who gave their lives for their country in the Great War.'

Soldier burials in the UK

Some village churchyards or cemeteries contain the graves of dead servicemen or women who had died of wounds or disease in hospitals in the UK, or died during training or as a result of an accident. Families were able to bring their bodies back home, hold funerals and tend their graves. The IWGC erected the same uniform headstones.

There are also over 30,000 soldier burials in the UK marked by individual headstones chosen by the family. When Harry Ayres' (see photo right) family were told that he had been seriously wounded, his mother set off for France to see him, where she found him in a dreadful state. She nagged officials and persuaded them to bring Harry back to a hospital in England, where, on his 18th birthday, he died of the head wounds he had suffered in France. His family were able to hold a funeral service and bury him in the local churchyard.

More recent memorials

After the Second World War, the names of dead servicemen were often added to existing memorials. In recognition of changing attitudes to conditions such as shell shock, the poignant Shot at Dawn Memorial at the National Memorial Arboretum in rural Staffordshire was unveiled in 2001. It commemorates 306 British and Commonwealth soldiers who were shot for desertion or cowardice during the First World War. They were all pardoned in 2006 in recognition of the fact that most of them were suffering from shell shock.

Until the Day breaks.

On that happy Easter morning
All the graves their dead restore;
Father, sister, child, and mother,
meet once more.

IN LOVING MEMORY OF

Bugler Harry Ayres,

Who died of wounds received in action, July 7th, 1915,

AGED 18 YEARS.

Bugler Harry Ayres and the mourning card sent out by his family. The Ayres family, probably with help from the wealthy local family where Harry worked as a footman before the war, erected a headstone of their own choice.

TOWN AND CITY WAR MEMORIALS

The citizens of towns and cities set about erecting memorials to the dead of their local community in the same way as people in rural areas – but often on a larger scale.

In Colchester, a garrison town in Essex, the war memorial committee included members of the town council, clergymen and army officers. They decided on a memorial designed by a sculptor called Henry Fehr that had been displayed along with other 'suitable' designs at the Royal Academy's War Memorial Exhibition in 1919. The memorial was unveiled in 1923 and includes three bronze statues: Victory, Saint George and Peace. With 1,203 dead from the town, their names appear on a roll of honour displayed in the nearby town hall rather than on the war memorial.

Towns across the British Empire were responding to the losses of the war. At Elora, a town in Ontario, Canada, there is a stone memorial (see photo, right) to the 20 men from the town who lost their lives thousands of miles from home fighting in the war.

Peace Memorial

In Watford, Hertfordshire, people decided to build a peace memorial rather than a war memorial. Money raised by the local community was mainly used to build the Watford and District Peace Memorial Hospital, opened in 1925. In 1928 a Peace Memorial was unveiled in front of the hospital gates comprising three bronze statues: To The Fallen, Victory and To the Wounded.

The Colchester War Memorial is dedicated both to the men who died and the men and women of the town who fought or carried out war work.

The Cenotaph in Elora, a town in the province of Ontario in Canada, commemorates the dead of both world wars.

TO·THE·MEN·OF·LIVERPOOL·WHO·FELL·IN·THE·GREAT·WAR

AND·ALL·WHO·HAVE·FALLEN·IN·CONFLICT·SINCE

AND·THE·VICTORY·THAT·DAY·WAS·TURNED·INTO·MOURNING·UNTO·ALL·THE·PEOPLE

The Liverpool Cenotaph

It took the citizens of Liverpool a long while to decide on how and where they would erect a war memorial to the 13,000 dead servicemen of the city, many of whom joined up in battalions known as the Liverpool Pals – groups of workmates or friends who joined up together. Unveiled on Armistice Day, 1930, it takes the form of a low altar decorated with bronze reliefs. The names of the dead servicemen are written on a roll of honour in Liverpool Town Hall and many of them are also remembered on numerous smaller memorials erected in schools, offices, factories and churches across the city.

After the war, workers in post offices, factories, banks, railway companies and other workplaces across the country raised money to set up memorials to their work colleagues who had died during the war. There are also war memorials in shops, fire stations and football stadiums.

The Liverpool Cenotaph, situated in front of St George's Hall, was unveiled in front of a huge crowd of 80,000 people in 1930. Bronze reliefs depict men marching off to war on one side and, here, mourners bringing wreaths on the other.

School war memorials

All through the war, school magazines printed obituaries of former pupils and after the war teachers and ex-pupils formed committees to create war memorials. Honour boards were a popular choice – wooden boards or stone panels – displaying the names of all who died, as well as new school buildings, swimming pools, libraries, rolls of honour or memorial windows, many of them still present in schools today.

National memorials

During the 1920s and 1930s, several vast monuments were raised to commemorate the sacrifice of different branches of the armed services or entire regiments. Regiments often decided on monuments or memorials in market towns and cities across the UK to which they had a particular link.

The Royal Regiment of Artillery eventually commissioned Charles Sergeant Jagger, a sculptor who had fought in the war, to design their memorial to the 49,076 men who had died in the war. Jagger created an immense Howitzer gun on a stone plinth, with carved reliefs showing scenes from the war. The memorial stands in Hyde Park, London, close to one commemorating the men of the Machine Gun Corps and two recent memorials erected by the New Zealand and Australian governments.

The First XV rugby team of Campbell College, Belfast photographed in 1914. Seven of these pupils and one teacher were dead by 1918, including Robert Semple (back row, second from left – and see page 5). The school war memorial lists the names of all 594 men who served in the armed forces, with the 126 who were killed listed on the central panel.

Four bronze statues of gunners stand on the plinth of the Royal Artillery Memorial in Hyde Park, London. Robert Semple's name (see above) is one of 49,076 names written on the roll of honour buried within the monument.

Panels around the base of the Royal Navy obelisk carry the names of 7,251 seamen from Britain, Australia and South Africa who sailed from Plymouth and died during the war.

Most of the seamen who died during the war were lost at sea. To commemorate their sacrifice, the Royal Navy decided to erect three identical memorials at the ports of Chatham, Portsmouth and Plymouth, where the majority of the seamen had boarded their ships. Robert Lorimer drew up the design creating a tall obelisk with four lions at its base. Bereaved relatives visited memorials such as this one to find the name of their dead son, husband or father inscribed in metal or stone for posterity.

In Scotland, talk of a national war memorial began in 1917 but it wasn't opened until 1927, after many struggles along the way. It takes the form of a shrine in Edinburgh Castle to the Scottish servicemen and women who died in the war. Over 147,000 names of the dead were written on a roll of honour and placed inside a casket inside the Hall of Honour, decorated by works of art depicting scenes from the war. It became a place of pilgrimage for grieving relatives who often visited on the anniversary of the death of their loved one.

On 5 March 1917, the British government approved the idea of a national war museum to record the events of the war when it was still going on. Its main aim was to record everyone's experience of the war – soldiers, sailors, airmen, civilians, munitions workers and children – individuals who had played their part in the Great War, as well as those who sacrificed their lives. In 1920, King George V officially opened the Imperial War Museum in London.

POPPIES

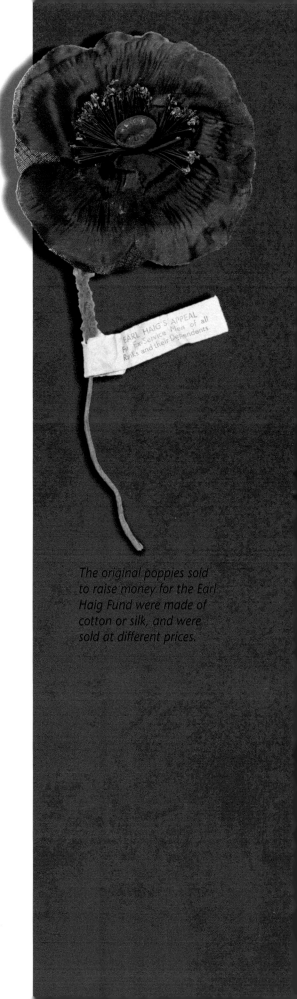

In the 1920s, people across the British Empire began to wear poppies in remembrance of those who had died during the war.

Bright red poppies were some of the only plants to grow in the battle-torn countryside of France and Belgium, a sight described by soldiers in their letters, diaries and poems. One such poem was written in 1915 by Major John McCrae, a doctor serving with the Canadian Overseas Expeditionary Force in Belgium. His now famous poem links the sadness of a friend dying with the poppies that grew on soldiers' graves and on the battlefields. It was published in *Punch* magazine in December 1915:

In Flanders fields the poppies blow
Between the crosses row on row,
That mark our place; and in the sky
The larks, still bravely singing, fly
Scarce heard amid the guns below.

We are the Dead. Short days ago
We lived, felt dawn, saw sunset glow,
Loved, and were loved, and now we lie
In Flanders Fields.

Take up our quarrel with the foe:
To you from failing hands we throw
The torch; be yours to hold it high.
If ye break faith with us who die
We shall not sleep, though poppies grow
In Flanders Fields.

The history of the poppy

Moina Michael, an American, read the poem in 1918 and decided to wear a paper poppy in remembrance of all those who died in the war. She campaigned for the poppy to be adopted as a national symbol of sacrifice in the USA.

The original poppies sold to raise money for the Earl Haig Fund were made of cotton or silk, and were sold at different prices.

DON'T FORGET

WEAR A WHITE POPPY FOR PEACE

Peace Pledge Union · 6 Endsleigh Street · London · WC1 0DX

The Peace Pledge Union continues to encourage people to wear a white poppy for peace on Remembrance Sunday. Some people choose to wear both a red poppy and a white poppy for peace on Armistice Day and Remembrance Sunday.

Blood Swept Lands and Seas of Red by Paul Cummins and Tom Piper.

Meanwhile in the United Kingdom, the Earl Haig Fund decided to sell cloth poppies to raise money for ex-servicemen and their families in 1921. The sale of the poppies raised over £100,000 so the British Legion set up a factory to produce its own poppies, staffed by disabled ex-servicemen. This work continues alongside the Lady Haig Poppy Factory established in Scotland.

In 1933 members of the Women's Co-operative Movement started to wear white poppies to show respect for the war dead but also reinforce the importance of peace at a time when tensions seemed to be building towards another large-scale war. The next year, the Peace Pledge Union began to distribute the white poppies to promote its message of peace.

Centenary commemoration

A hundred years after the war began, artists Paul Cummins and Tom Piper created their art installation *Blood Swept Lands and Seas of Red* in the moat of the Tower of London. Between 17 July and 11 November 2014, 888,246 ceramic poppies were planted to represent every British military death during the war. Crowds flocked to see it and the sale of the ceramic poppies raised money for the British Legion and other charities.

Acts of remembrance, past and present

Known as the Great War at the time, everyone hoped that there would never be another war like it. Sadly, 21 years later, another major conflict broke out, now known as the Second World War. People continue to remember the dead of both world wars and other conflicts using many of the traditions established after the First World War.

RESEARCHING THE DEAD OF THE FIRST WORLD WAR

Here are some tips on how to find out more about someone who died during the First World War.

To start your search, find out as much as you can about the person. Copy down their name as fully as possible, including any initials or anything that indicates which rank and/or military unit they belonged to. The service number will help narrow down your searches. This number appeared on official documents, identification tags (worn around the neck and wrist) and was sometimes included on letters home. If you are researching a woman, find out whether they were with the Women's Army Auxiliary Corps (later renamed the Queen Mary's Army Auxiliary Corps), Queen Alexandra's Imperial Military Nursing Service or the Voluntary Aid Detachment.

This identification tag stamped with Rifleman Maurice Baker's service number was worn around his wrist. He also wore an identification disc on a leather cord around his neck.

If you are researching a dead relative, ask around the family to see if anyone has photos, medals, letters, official documents or any other memorabilia that they can show you. If you are lucky, someone in your family may have already started doing some research.

Commonwealth War Graves Commission

Armed with this information, log on to the Commonwealth War Graves Commission website:

www.cwgc.org/find-war-dead.aspx

This free-to-view database lists the names and the places of commemoration of Commonwealth forces who died in both world wars, as well as nurses and women serving with the Women's Army Auxiliary Corps and men who died serving in the Chinese Labour Corps.

This is the type of information you will be able to discover on their site: I entered the name of Robert Semple, pictured here. The CWGC datebase brought up five Robert Semples. As I knew that he was in the Royal Field Artillery I was able to narrow down the search results to the correct one: Robert Edward Watson Semple. The database also gave me this information: his rank of Captain, his date of death (5 November 1918), his age – 22, confirmed his regiment, and told me that he is buried in St Sever Cemetery Extension, Rouen, France with grave reference S V G 12. The database also gave me his parents' names and address and that he won the Military Cross. By clicking on the name of the cemetery, I could access information about the location, history and opening times of this CWGC-maintained cemetery extension.

The War Graves Photographic Project

The CWGC database carries a link to The War Graves Photographic Project website: **www.twgpp.org/**

This database is still growing and features photographs of individual graves in CWGC cemeteries across the world.

Pay-to-view websites

If you want to find out more, there are several pay-to-view websites, such as **www.ancestry.co.uk**. Your local library or school may have a subscription to the Ancestry website. Ancestry and other similar sites hold this type of information:

- British army medal index cards – these give details of service medals awarded posthumously;
- naval casualties;
- Royal Flying Corps/Royal Air Force muster roll (April 1918);
- information about prisoners of war;
- soldiers' wills;
- British army service records (although some of these were destroyed by an air raid during the Second World War);
- British army pension records;
- Graves Registration Reports and Burial Registers;
- 1911 Census as well as Birth, Marriage and Death certificates;
- Soldiers Died in the Great War – brief details of over 700,000 deaths of the war;

- Silver War Badge records (the Silver War Badge was given to men who had served overseas but had been discharged from the armed forces due to injury or illness);
- Unit War Diaries.

Regimental museums and newspapers

In addition, many regiments have a regimental museum and archive. Regimental histories were produced shortly after the war and provide much information about the progress of the war as it affected the battalions of a particular regiment. Your local library service should be able to order up the relevant regimental history. For information about the award of medals and for brief details of men who were killed, search the website of the *London Gazette*. Local newspapers at the time printed obituaries of those who died during the war.

Researching a nurse

To research a nurse, the Scarlet Finders website can navigate you through the process: **www.scarletfinders.co.uk**

Nursing service records and campaign medal records can also be accessed through pay-to-view websites, such as Ancestry (see page 44) and you could also find out whether the Red Cross holds any information by following this link: **www.redcross.org.uk/About-us/Who-we-are/Museum-and-archives/Resources-for-researchers**

Imperial War Museums

IWM represents all the experiences of war, both military and civilian. Visit the museums and/or their website which includes many fascinating articles about different aspects of the First World War. They have also put together useful information about how to trace your family history at: **www.iwm.org.uk/collections-research/tracing-your-family-history**

War memorials

Looking at information linked to war memorials can reward you with more information than you might expect. The UK War Memorials Archive can be accessed using this link. **www.iwm.org.uk/warmemorials**

Look up war memorials linked to a particular place and find out when they were erected, how many people they commemorate, what they look like, how much they originally cost and other fascinating details. To read details of the names inscribed on the war memorials, look at the Royal British Legion 'Roll of Honour' at: **www.roll-of-honour.com**

You can look up places by county and then by village or town. For instance, if you enter 'Suffolk' and then 'Lavenham' you can read the names of all the men listed on Lavenham Church's war memorial (see photo page 29), with short biographical details.

The War Memorials Trust administers grants to maintain war memorials and keeps records of those that it has helped to preserve. It also has a useful document with tips on how to research the names on a war memorial, accessed by using this link: **www.warmemorials.org/uploads/publications/123.pdf**

The Irish War Memorials Project is a developing site that is producing an inventory of war memorials in the Republic of Ireland and Northern Ireland at: **www.irishwarmemorials.ie/**

At the Scottish National War Memorial website: **www.snwm.org/** you can read about the history of this national war memorial for Scotland and also look at their roll of honour for both world wars.

Of course you might not know whether the person you are researching appears on a war memorial. Use what information you know about them already to search war memorials linked to their birthplace or where they were living when they joined the armed forces. Alongside church and chapel war memorials, they were also erected in other places, including post offices, factories, railway stations, police stations, hospitals, schools, universities – anywhere where a group of people wanted to commemorate those who had died.

Local historians and other individuals have often researched the names on a war memorial and this information can be accessed with the use of a reliable search engine. For instance, interesting information about Captain Robert Semple (see photo) can be discovered by using the Internet to look at information linked to the war memorials in St Michael's Church, Woburn Sands and St Saviour's Church, St Albans. His parents lived in both places during and after the war, so he appears on both memorials, as well as on the honour board of his school, Campbell College, Belfast, Northern Ireland.

Finally, there is a wealth of information about the First World War that can be accessed on the Internet, including the excellent 'The Long, Long Trail' website (**www.1914–1918.net/**), and there are shelves of fascinating books about the war in libraries and bookshops. To read more about the history of the Commonwealth War Graves Commission, read *Remembered: The History of the Commonwealth War Graves Commission* by Julie Summers and *Empires of the Dead* by David Crane.

GLOSSARY

armed forces The collective term for a country's army, navy and air force.

Armistice An agreement signed by all sides fighting in the First World War to stop fighting at 11 o'clock on 11 November, 1918, and start working out a peace treaty.

Armistice Balls Parties attended by survivors of the war and others to celebrate the end of the war. They were held on the anniversary of the Armistice (11 November) and had largely died out by the end of the 1920s.

Armistice Day Today Armistice Day is also known as Remembrance Day and occurs on 11 November each year. Ceremonies occur at war memorials and in churches and chapels throughout the country to remember those who have died in all conflicts, not just the First World War. For many people, Remembrance Sunday services and other acts of commemoration have taken over from Armistice Day.

Army Labour Corps The organisation formed in 1917 to take on the work of building trenches, maintaining roads, railways and canals and transporting equipment and supplies, amongst other vital tasks, during the war.

artillery Large guns that fire explosive shells over long distances.

Baker, Sir Herbert (1862–1946) An eminent architect who advised the IWGC on designs for its military cemeteries, including the design for Tyne Cot Cemetery in Belgium.

battalion An army unit made up of about 800–1,000 soldiers.

Battle of Loos This battle fought between 25 September and 18 October was a British attempt to break the deadlock of trench warfare on the Western Front.

Battle of the Somme A battle fought between 1 July and 18 November by British and French armies to break the deadlock of trench warfare on the Western Front.

Battle of Verdun One of the costliest wars of the First World War in terms of lives lost, this battle was fought between 21 February and 20 December 1916 between the French and German armies, centred on the French town of Verdun.

bereaved People who have recently experienced the death of a close relative or friend.

Binyon, Laurence (1869–1943) Laurence Binyon worked as the Keeper of Prints and Drawings at the British Museum for 40 years but was also a published poet and art historian.

Blomfield, Sir Reginald (1856–1942) Reginald Blomfield was an architect, garden designer and author who became one of the chief architects involved with the design of IWGC cemeteries. He designed the Cross of Sacrifice and the Menin Gate Memorial, amongst others.

blueprint Something which acts as a template for others.

British Empire Countries ruled from Britain, which in 1914 included India as well as the self-governing nations within the British Commonwealth, such as Canada, Australia, New Zealand, South Africa and Newfoundland.

British Legion This association was formed in 1921 for the support of former members of the armed forces and their dependents. British Legion Clubs in villages and towns across the country were social clubs where veterans of the war could meet.

Canadian Overseas Expeditionary Force Of the 630,000 Canadians who served in the First World War, 424,000 went overseas and were thus part of the Canadian Overseas Expeditionary Force.

Captain During the First World War a captain commanded a company of between 120 and 200 men.

carved relief A type of stone carving where the design stands out from the surface of the stone.

Cenotaph The war memorial designed for the Peace Day events of July 1919 by Sir Edwin Lutyens. Originally made in plaster and wood, it was remade in stone and unveiled on Armistice Day (11 November) 1920.

Chinese Labour Corps Men from China were recruited during 1916 as a labour force to carry out work such as the building and repair of railways, docks and trenches. They also worked to clear the battlefields after the war. Around 1,900 Chinese workers died, many of them from disease.

Commonwealth War Graves Commission The Imperial War Graves Commission, established by Royal Charter in May 1917 to care for the war dead, was renamed as the Commonwealth War Graves Commission in 1960.

Cross of Sacrifice The stone cross designed by Sir Reginald Blomfield which stands in CWGC cemeteries with over 40 graves.

curator A keeper or custodian of a museum or other collection.

Fallen, the The dead of the First World War came to be known as 'the Fallen' which is perhaps a 'softer' way of saying that they had died.

fiancé A man to whom a woman is engaged to be married.

field hospital The Royal Army Medical Corps established permanent base hospitals as well as temporary field hospitals in the war zones. Nurses, doctors and surgeons attended the wounded in field hospitals of various types that were usually set up in tents and could be moved if the front line moved forwards or back.

Field marshal The highest rank of officer in the British army.

front line The trench that was closest to the enemy.

Graves Concentration Units The part of the IWGC that worked under the authority of the army to help clear the battlefields of bodies.

Graves Registration Commission The part of the IWGC responsible for registering the location, identity and other information related to each burial.

Great War People alive at the time referred to the First World War as the 'Great War' until another world war broke out in 1939.

gun salute A gesture of respect to an individual that takes the form of firing off rifles or guns.

headstone A slab of stone set up at the head of a grave.

honour board Here, the name for the wooden memorials set up in schools and other institutions listing those who had served and/or died in the First World War.

Howitzer A gun used for firing explosive shells.

identification disc/identity tag Military identity tags or identification discs were supposed to be worn by members of the armed services at all times to aid identification should they be injured or killed. Each tag was stamped with the name, service number and faith of the wearer.

Imperial War Graves Commission The Commission was established by Royal Charter in May 1917 to care for graves and memorials to the war dead.

Jagger, Charles Sergeant (1885–1934) An eminent British sculptor who gave up his studies to fight in the British army. After the war, he sculpted many war memorials, including the Royal Artillery Memorial.

Jekyll, Gertrude (1843–1932) Gertrude Jekyll was a leading garden designer who advised the IWGC on garden design and planting.

Kenyon, Sir Frederic (1963–1952) Director of the British Museum, Kenyon drew together the visions of the different architects that had been asked to provide designs and ideas by the IWGC.

Kipling, Rudyard (1865–1936) The writer and poet, Rudyard Kipling, became the literary advisor to the IWGC. His only son, John, died at the Battle of Loos.

Last Post In 1928 members of the local fire brigade in Ypres, Belgium, decided to mark the sacrifice of the men who had died during the First World War by establishing the tradition of the Last Post – buglers sounding out the Last Post and the Reveille. Since 11 November 1929 the ceremony has taken place every evening, apart from during the Second World War.

Lorimer, Sir Robert (1864–1929) The Scottish architect, Sir Robert Lorimer, designed the Scottish National War Memorial in Edinburgh Castle as well as the overall design of IWGC cemeteries in Italy and Greece.

Lutyens, Sir Edwin (1869–1944) This influential architect was involved in the design and layout of IWGC cemeteries. In addition he designed the Cenotaph, the Thiepval Memorial to the Missing and many others.

memorial plaque A memorial plaque, scroll and the King's message were sent out to the immediate next-of-kin of those who died serving in the British and Empire forces during the First World War.

messenger boy The Post Office employed messenger boys to deliver telegrams.

mourning card A mourning card was sent out by a bereaved person to announce the death of their loved one to family and friends.

next-of-kin A person's closest living relative or relatives, such as their parents, wife or sibling.

obelisk A tapering stone pillar set up as a monument or a landmark.

obituary A printed notice of someone's death, often including biographical details.

ossuary A room or hall filled with the bones of dead people.

Peace Day A national day of celebration on on 19 July 1919 to mark the signing of the peace treaty on 28 June 1919.

pilgrimage A journey to a place of significance. In this instance, pilgrims went to visit the graves, memorials and battlefields of the First World War.

pocket book During the war, many men serving in the armed forces kept a small notebook called a pocket book inside the pocket of their uniform. Wills, letters from loved ones and even photographs were kept safe, folded inside.

rank A position in the hierarchy of the armed forces, such as private, second lieutenant, captain or general.

Red Cross An international organisation that works to relieve suffering, whether due to a natural disaster or a war. During the First World War, the Red Cross and its volunteers nursed the wounded, carried out air raid duty, tracked down missing people and transported the wounded in their own fleet of ambulances.

regiment The basic administration unit of the British army, divided into several battalions.

Remembrance Sunday The second Sunday in November, the Sunday nearest to 11 November, Armistice Day, when the dead of both world wars and later conflicts are commemorated.

repatriation To bring back a person or a corpse to their home country.

roll of honour A list of people whose actions are honoured. During the First World War communities decided to create a roll of honour listing those who were serving in the war. After the war, rolls of honour usually listed those who had died in the war, or all those who had served as well as those who had died.

Royal Charter A formal document issued by the king or queen to establish an organisation.

Saint Barnabas Society The society was founded in 1919 to help the bereaved to visit the graves of their loved ones.

Saint George The patron saint of England.

sapper A soldier responsible for building bridges, laying and clearing mines and other tasks.

shrine A place of reverence associated with particular people or with a saint.

Stone of Remembrance The stone memorial designed by Sir Edwin Lutyens that can be seen in CWGC cemeteries containing more than 1,000 dead.

telegram A message sent by telegraph machine and then delivered in written or printed form.

unidentified soldier Because of the nature of the First World War, many dead soldiers' corpses lost all identifying features and it became impossible to name them.

Voluntary Aid Detachment/VAD A volunteer nurse serving in the Voluntary Aid Detachment.

War Office The part of the British government responsible for the British army.

Ware, Sir Fabian (1869–1949) Sir Fabian Ware was instrumental in the formation of the Imperial, later Commonwealth, War Graves Commission.

Western Front The zone of fighting in Belgium and France that ran from the Belgian coast to the Swiss border.

Women's Army Auxiliary Corps/ WAAC The WAAC was established in 1916 so that women could perform tasks that had been undertaken by soldiers, thus allowing more fighting men to reach the front line trenches.

wreath An arrangement of flowers, leaves and stems laid on a grave as a mark of respect.

Further reading

Here is a list of a few novels and memoirs written by individuals who served in the First World War:

All Quiet on the Western Front by Erich Maria Remarque
Goodbye to All That by Robert Graves
Memoirs of an Infantry Officer by Siegfried Sassoon
Storm of Steel by Ernst Jünger
Testament of Youth by Vera Brittain
Undertones of War by Edmund Blunden.

INDEX